Cape Town

A VISUAL CELEBRATION

Cape Town

A VISUAL CELEBRATION

PETER JOYCE

Struik Publishers (Pty) Ltd
(A member of Struik New Holland Publishing (Pty) Ltd)
Cornelis Struik House
80 McKenzie Street
Cape Town 8001

Reg. No.: 54/00965/07

First edition 1998

Designer Janice Evans
Design assistant Lellyn Creamer
Managing editor Annlerie van Rooyen
Editor Alfred LeMaitre
Cartographers Mark Seabrook and John Loubser
Reproduction by Hirt & Carter Cape (Pty) Ltd
Printed and bound by Tien Wah Press (Pte) Limited, Singapore

2 4 6 8 10 9 7 5 3 1

ISBN 1 86872 154 X

Cover: The Atlantic seaboard at Clifton; **Back Cover** (clockwise from top left): Architecture on Long Street; New Year 'Coon' Carnival; Table Mountain cable car; city centre produce vendor; **Spine:** scarlet-breasted sunbird; **Front flap:** Table Mountain from Signal Hill; **Back flap:** Victoria Wharf V&A Waterfront; **Half title:** Old Port Captain's Building, V&A Waterfront; **Title page:** Table Mountain viewed from Bloubergstrand; **Imprint page:** Trek fisherman, False Bay coast; **Contents page:** Muslim Kramat on Signal Hill.

CONTENTS

Introduction

The vistas from the straight-edge crest of Table Mountain are quite breathtaking, especially in that magical late-afternoon hour when the dying sun softens and deepens the colours of earth and sky. A spectacular highland ridge, the 'spine' of the Cape Peninsula, runs away to the south to end in the massive headland of Cape Point. To the east is the broad blue sweep of False Bay, its waters girded by golden sands; to the west the Twelve Apostles, a regiment of high pinnacles and buttresses that stands guard over the Atlantic seaboard. Look north, beyond the

docklands of Table Bay and you'll see Robben Island, notorious for its role in political history and now a nature reserve, museum and memorial to South Africa's liberation struggle.

Directly below the heights, lying snugly in the amphitheatre formed by the mountain, its flanking peaks and the sea, is the city itself, trim, stylish, even beautiful in this most magnificent of settings. By international standards it is a small metropolis – the central area covers just a score or so of blocks – but the wider area is substantial enough: more than three million people live in the suburbs shadowed by the upland range and in the north and east, on the great, windblown plain known as the Cape Flats.

Cape Town, the country's 'mother city', legislative capital and third largest conurbation (after Johannesburg and Durban), was founded in the 1650s by a small party of Dutch settlers sent to establish a halfway station on the sea lanes between Europe and Holland's Eastern possessions. Their leader, Jan van Riebeeck, had been instructed 'to erect defences, and to secure herbs, flesh, water and other needful refreshments' for the passing fleets of the Dutch East India Company. At that time, and for centuries before, the Cape Peninsula and its hinterland were home to groups of Khoikhoi, a semi-nomadic people closely related to the

Above: The harbour and city at dusk. Cape Town was founded, in the 1650s, as a halfway station on the trade route between Europe and the East Indies, and it remains a major maritime centre.
Right: Poised between Table Mountain and the Atlantic shoreline, the exclusive suburb of Clifton presents a magical sight as evening descends.

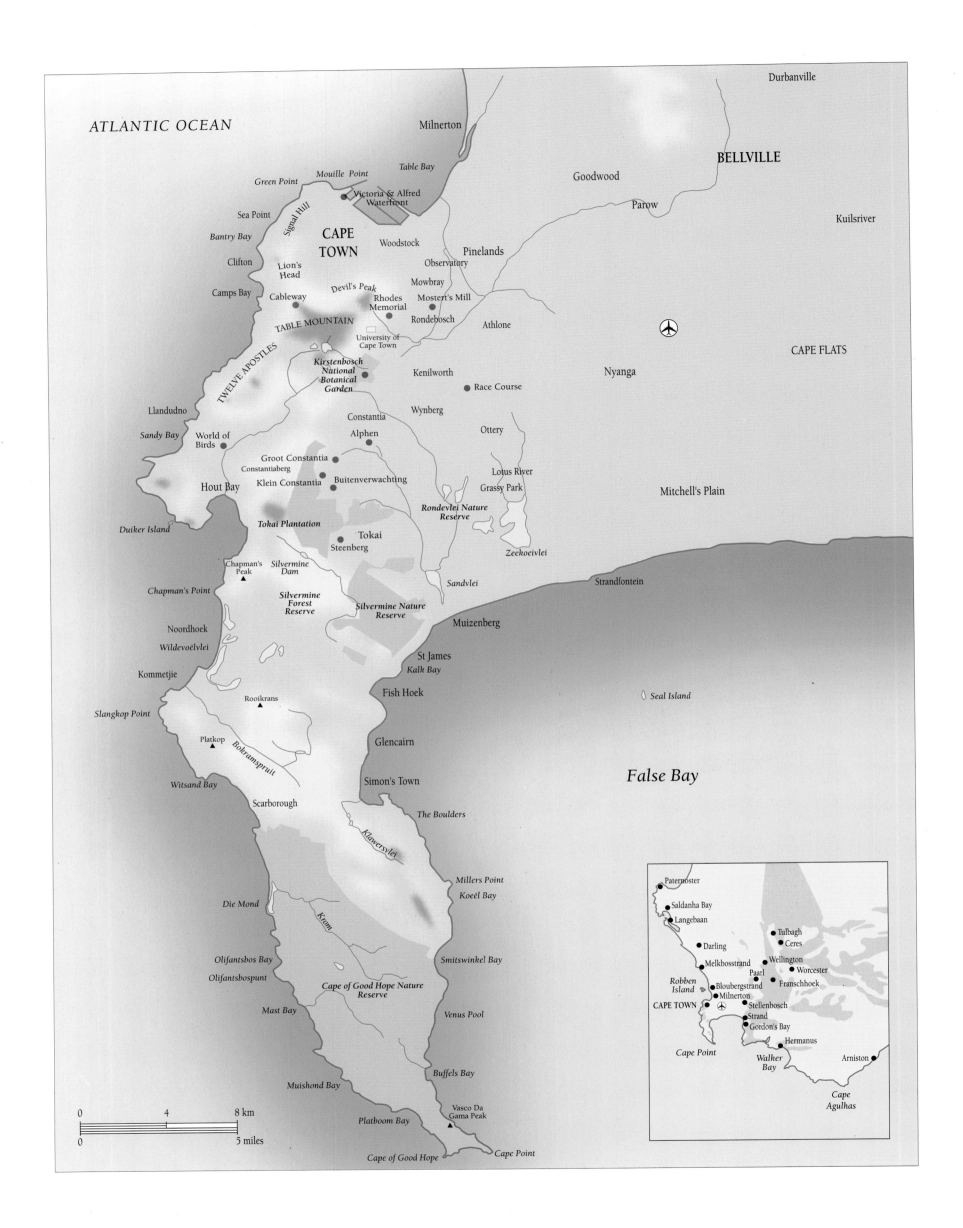

ATLANTIC OCEAN

Durbanville

Milnerton

BELLVILLE

Table Bay

Goodwood

Mouille Point

Green Point

Victoria & Alfred
Waterfront

Sea Point

Signal Hill

Bantry Bay

Clifton

Lion's
Head

CAPE
TOWN

Woodstock

Devil's Peak

Camps Bay

Cableway

TABLE MOUNTAIN

TWELVE APOSTLES

Llandudno

Sandy Bay

World of
Birds

Groot Constantia

Constantiaberg

Klein Constantia

Hout Bay

Duiker Island

Tokai Plantation

Tokai

Steenberg

Chapman's
Peak

Silvermine
Dam

Chapman's Point

Silvermine
Forest
Reserve

Silvermine Nature
Reserve

Noordhoek

Wildevoëlvlei

Kommetjie

Rooikrans

Slangkop Point

Platkop

Bokramspruit

Witsand Bay

Scarborough

Die Mond

Krom

Olifantsbos Bay

Olifantsbospunt

Cape of Good Hope Nature
Reserve

Mast Bay

Muishond Bay

Platboom Bay

Cape of Good Hope

Parow

Kuilsriver

Pinelands

Observatory

Mowbray

Rhodes
Memorial

Mostert's Mill

Rondebosch

Athlone

University of
Cape Town

CAPE FLATS

Kirstenbosch
National
Botanical
Garden

Kenilworth

Nyanga

Race Course

Wynberg

Constantia

Alphen

Ottery

Lotus River

Buitenverwachting

Grassy Park

Mitchell's Plain

Rondevlei Nature
Reserve

Zeekoeivlei

Sandvlei

Strandfontein

Muizenberg

St James

Kalk Bay

Fish Hoek

Seal Island

Glencairn

Simon's Town

False Bay

The Boulders

Millers Point

Koeël Bay

Smitswinkel Bay

Venus Pool

Buffels Bay

Vasco Da
Gama Peak

Cape Point

0   4   8 km

0   5 miles

Paternoster

Saldanha Bay

Langebaan

Tulbagh

Ceres

Darling

Wellington

Melkbosstrand

Worcester

Paarl

Robben
Island

Blaauwbergstrand

Franschhoek

Milnerton

CAPE TOWN

Stellenbosch

Strand

Gordon's Bay

Cape Point

Hermanus

Walker
Bay

Arniston

Cape
Agulhas

Bushmen (or San) of the interior. Perhaps surprisingly the two communities, European and African, lived in reasonable harmony for a time but, with the expansion of the colony the Khoikhoi were dispossessed of their traditional grazing lands and this, compounded by devastating smallpox epidemics, destroyed much of their cultural identity.

Meanwhile, slaves were arriving in the colony in increasing numbers, some from other parts of Africa, the majority Malay-speaking folk from the Indies, devout Muslims who brought much-needed skills into the rugged little settlement. Europe, however, remained the major source of immigration in the early years, producing a steady trickle of Dutch, Scandinavians, Germans and, from the 1680s, Huguenot refugees from a France torn by religious strife. And then, at the end of the 1700s, British troops invaded the Cape to inaugurate a long period of 'anglicization'. The final threads in Cape Town's human fabric were woven in during the 20th century by poverty-stricken Xhosa-speaking migrants from rural areas of the Eastern Cape.

Over the centuries, Cape Town has grown into a cosmopolitan, lively place of modest skyscrapers, animated thoroughfares, leafy piazzas, markets and gleaming malls, the whole swept by the clean winds of the southern seas. Reminders of the past are everywhere. In the heart of the city, flanked by stately and historic buildings, is the Company's Garden, the original site of the Dutch East India Company's vegetable gardens and now a lush and attractive urban park. Within the Company's Garden lie

Above: The face of innocence: a young Capetonian campaigns in support of the city's ultimately unsuccessful Olympic bid. *Below:* The stately Mount Nelson Hotel has hosted the world's notables for the past century; among its earliest guests was a young Winston Churchill. *Overleaf:* A bird's-eye view of central Cape Town, embraced by majestic Table Mountain and its flanking arms.

the South African Museum and Planetarium, which displays natural and ethnographic treasures, and the South African National Gallery, one of the country's premier art collections. Both institutions are important storehouses of South Africa's cultural heritage.

The oldest of Cape Town's edifices is the massive-walled, pentagonal Castle of Good Hope, completed in 1676; the most beautiful perhaps Koopmans-De Wet House in Strand Street, a classic example of late 18th-century Cape domestic architecture, and Groot Constantia, one of the grandest of many mansions built in the distinctive Cape Dutch rural style. Scores of other, equally charming structures have survived the decades, among them whitewashed homesteads with enormous teak doors, green-shuttered windows and vined courtyards; Georgian and Regency residences; Victorian shops and cottages trimmed with fanciful wrought ironwork, and much else.

History and architecture, though, are only two among many elements that make Cape Town such a pleasant place to visit. The magnificence of the Peninsula's scenery and its unique plant life; the green valleys and vineyards of the hinterland; Cape Point and the lovely gardens of Kirstenbosch; the coasts, their beaches, bays and fishing harbours; the exuberance of the Waterfront; the calendar of arts; the myriad eating and drinking places – each is a compelling attraction in itself. Together, they provide Capetonians with a seductively pleasant environment, and the traveller with a very special destination.

Opposite: The gardens of Kirstenbosch, among the world's most important botanical treasure houses, nurture more than 9 000 species of indigenous plants. The gardens sprawl over 530 hectares (1 310 acres) of Table Mountain's well-watered southern slopes. *Above*: Cable cars carry visitors on a thrilling ride to the summit of Table Mountain. *Below*: The equestrian statue of 'Physical Energy' at Rhodes Memorial.

Mountain Majesty

Perhaps the most enduring image of Cape Town is that of a neat city dominated, almost overwhelmed, by the awe-inspiring splendour of Table Mountain. But this great massif is only one (albeit the most monumental) among a striking array of highland features, the northern extremity of a hilly 'spine' that runs down the length of the Peninsula to end at the dramatic cliffs of Cape Point. The heights, usually standing clear against the blueness of the sky but sometimes shrouded in low clouds brought in by the summer south-easterly and by the rain-bearing

winter winds, have many faces, many moods, their colours and character changing with the seasons. They are always, though, lovely to behold, a magnet for hikers, climbers, ramblers and lovers of nature at its grandest.

The uplands are especially notable for the variety of their plant life: Table Mountain alone, its slopes and high central plateau, sustains nearly 2 000 different indigenous species – more than are found in the whole of the United Kingdom. They are part of what is known as the Cape Floral Kingdom, a quite remarkable botanical zone that occupies less than one tenth of one percent of the earth's land area, yet is so richly endowed that it enjoys equal status with the vast Boreal Kingdom that covers North America and most of Europe and Asia. Collectively, they belong to the 'fynbos' ('fine bush') biome and, for the most part, comprise hardy, drought-resistant, small-leafed plants such as the proteas and ericas. Like so many other elements of South Africa's priceless natural heritage these uplands and their plant cover are under pressure, the environment threatened by the encroachment of alien flora and an increasingly intrusive human presence. The future, though, holds promise: Table Mountain and its neighbours provide the cornerstones of the recently proclaimed Cape Peninsula National Park which, with luck, goodwill and good management, will preserve the integrity and beauty of this small corner of the country for generations to come.

Above: This delicate pincushion protea is one of Table Mountain's myriad floral species, many of which are unique to the Peninsula. *Right:* Banks of spring flowers on Signal Hill counterpoint the awe-inspiring starkness of Table Mountain's northern face.

The view of the city and Table Bay from the cable car is truly stupendous. Most of the mountain's visitors make their way to the summit by cable car, a comfortable five-minute trip – and a safe one: there has never been a serious accident in more than half a century of operation.

Looking towards Lion's Head, the conical peak that guards Table Mountain's western flank. The summit of Lion's Head is a fairly easy climb, and affords superb views of the city, harbour and bay below.

At twilight, shadows transform Table Mountain, etching every buttress and ridge line. *Opposite:* Only the cableway station breaks the smooth summit line of the precipitous northern face. *Above:* Moonrise over the western slopes of the mountain, looking towards the fashionable suburb of Camps Bay. *Left:* Bare-crested Lion's Head rises 670 metres (2 010 feet) above the Atlantic seaboard.

Left: Table Bay in the stillness of evening, with Milnerton Lagoon in the foreground, Table Mountain providing the backdrop. The bay is not always so tranquil; scores of ships have foundered in its waters. *Overleaf, top:* A mountain lookout provides a panoramic view of sprawling suburbs and distant mountain ramparts. Perhaps the best time to make the ascent is late afternoon – to catch the sunset and deepening colours of sky and land. Development at the summit has been kept to a bare minimum; the cableway station, restaurant and souvenir shop have been carefully designed to blend with their surroundings. *Overleaf, bottom*: The classic Cape Town cityscape – a view that lingers in the minds of those who arrive by sea.

Right: Short trails meander across the mountain-top plateau. These are, for the most part, fairly gentle walks, but some of the steeper scrambles and climbs call for nerve, skill and a good sense of direction. The weather on and around the summit can be treacherous and, when it takes a turn for the worse (which it sometimes does with dramatic suddenness), one can easily lose one's way. *Overleaf:* With their fine leaves and voluptuous flowers, the tough, hardy proteas that decorate the slopes of Table Mountain are among the Peninsula's most arresting sights.

The mountain's flora and fauna includes pretty mesembryanthemums (*top*), a showy locust (*above centre*) and the endearing dassie (*above*). *Right:* A plethora of indigenous plants, including leucadendrons and reedlike restios, flourish among the rocks. *Overleaf:* Table Mountain's aspect changes by the hour: at dusk, a shadowy presence (*top left*); at midday, a stark sentinel (*bottom left*). Its heights are often obscured by the billowing clouds of the famous 'tablecloth' (*top right*); early morning light mellows the crags (*bottom right*).

Among the finest of scenic routes is that along the Peninsula's western or Atlantic seaboard. *Previous pages*: From Camps Bay to Llandudno, the coast road winds along the foot of the mighty Twelve Apostles (there are in fact 17 of these towering buttresses). *Left*: Even more spectacular is Chapman's Peak Drive, which at one point cuts through cliffs that plunge sheer down to the sea 600 metres (1,800 feet) below. The vistas here are breathtaking, as are those along the Ou Kaapse Weg, or the Old Cape Road (*above*), which leads over the Steenberg range, and affords fine views across False Bay towards the distant Hottentots-Holland range. *Overleaf*: The lower portion of the Peninsula mountain chain runs south-eastward to Cape Point. The fishing village of Kommetjie is in the foreground.

City of Colour & Contrast

Cape Town's compact and attractive centre is easy to navigate and well worth taking the time to explore. A good place to begin, perhaps, is in Adderley Street, named after an obscure 19th-century British politician who helped halt a scheme, designed on Australian lines, to send British convicts to the Cape. It is now the city's principal thoroughfare, its northern end leading into the attractive, rather stately

Heerengracht, its southern curving past the compact, Gothic-style St George's Anglican cathedral, with its lovely Rose Window. Parallel to Adderley Street is the pedestrian-only St George's Mall, a six-block stretch perfect for enjoying the sights and sounds of street performers and browsing through the wares of the many craft and curio vendors.

Beyond is the Company's Garden, also called the Gardens, originally laid out to provide food for the first colonists and their seagoing brethren. Over the years its function changed, and by the end of the 18th century much of it had been given over to beautiful and (some of them) rare plants, its broad avenues lined with oak, ash, lemon, olive and orange trees, guavas, cherries, pears and apples. Around it stand a clutch of splendid buildings, among them the Houses of Parliament, the Tuynhuis, the Old and the Great Synagogues, the National Gallery, the South African Museum and Planetarium and the South African Library.

On the slopes of Signal Hill is the Bo-Kaap ('Above the Cape'), home to a section of the region's Muslim community. Many of the residents are descendants of slaves brought in by the Dutch. The Bo-Kaap is a charming place of minareted mosques and flat-roofed houses, and it presents another face of a city remarkable for the diversity of its cultures.

The oldest of Cape Town's buildings is the five-sided Castle of Good Hope, completed in the 1670s for defence against threats from the sea. Its precincts now serve, for the most part, as a museum. *Above*: One of the Castle's sun-dappled flagstone passageways. *Right*: Careful restoration work has made the Dolphin Pool one of the Castle's loveliest spots.

At night, the lights of Cape Town transform office towers into beacons (**top**),
and add excitement to Long Street's
trendy cafés (**centre**) and the nightclubs
clustered on lower Loop Street (**above**).
Right: Dwarfed by the towers of the central business district, the Lutheran
Church on Strand Street anchors a group
of historic structures.

Service with a smile. Flower and fresh produce sellers are a traditional and attractive part of the city scene; the flower sellers in Adderley Street and the Grand Parade are especially well known, while fruit and vegetable stalls throughout the city offer the bounty of the surrounding farmlands.

Above: Church Street's sidewalk cafés allow visitors to savour one of the city's quieter and more pleasant corners. A pedestrian-only section of Church Street is also the venue of a regular antiques market. *Opposite*: Perhaps the most pleasing of the city's plazas is Greenmarket Square, a shady, cobblestoned area crammed with traders' stalls that stock everything from household junk to stylish jewellery. The steeple at top right belongs to the Metropolitan Methodist Church, whose foundation stone was laid in 1876. Across the street stands the Old Town House, which originally (from the 1750s) accommodated the Burgher Senate – the civic council – and now serves as an art gallery housing Dutch and Flemish masterpieces.

Opposite: The weekly market at the Grand Parade is one of Cape Town's liveliest emporia, with fabrics of all types a speciality. In the background is Cape Town City Hall, an Italian Renaissance-style edifice built in the early years of the 20th century. *Above and left*: Craftwork of all kinds features among the wares offered by traders in Greenmarket Square and elsewhere in the city.

Top: Oak-lined Government Avenue invites visitors to stroll in the Company's Garden. *Above*: Part of Government Avenue is flanked by the Houses of Parliament. *Right*: A monument to statesman Jan Smuts stands outside the South African National Gallery. *Far right*: A memorial honours the heroism of South African troops during the First World War; in the background is the popular South African Museum.

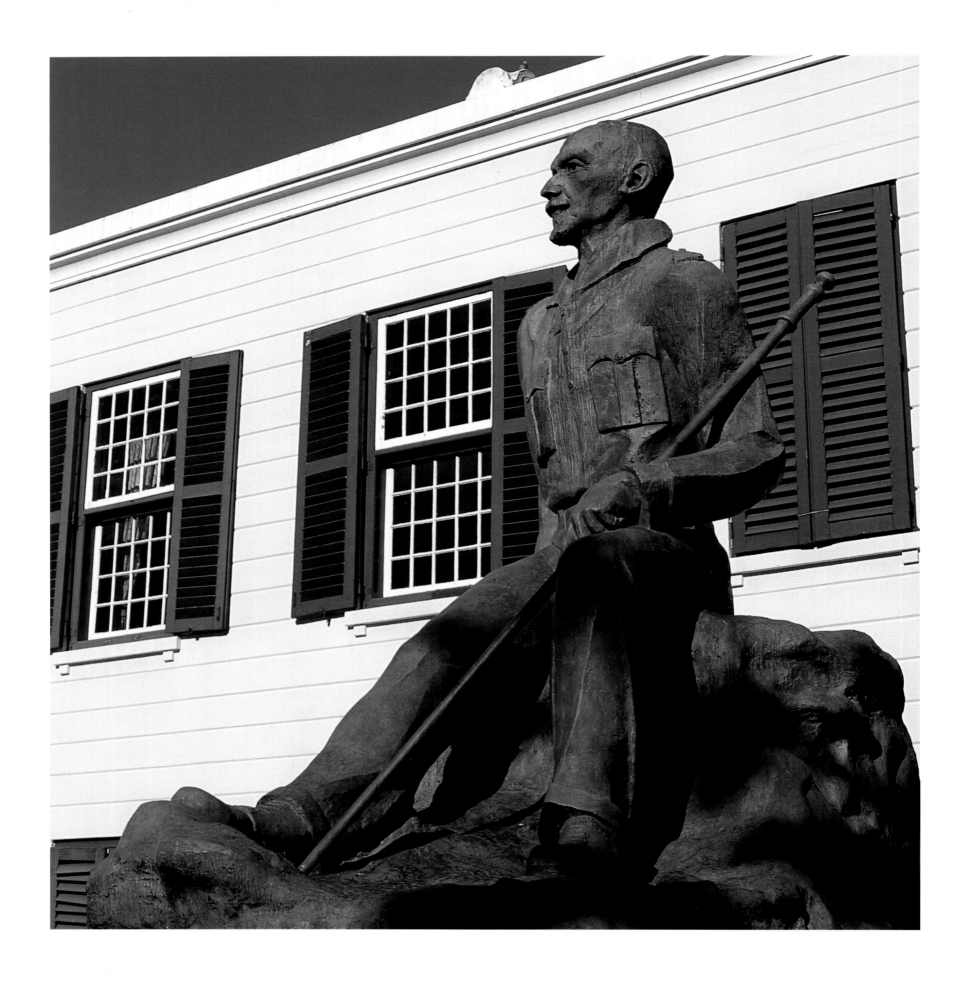

Above: A modestly impressive statue of Jan Smuts, soldier, politician, philosopher and, arguably, the most respected South African statesman of the old order, surveys Adderley Street. Behind the statue is the Cultural History Museum, housed in what was originally the Dutch East India Company's slave quarters. *Opposite*: An essay in contrasts – 19th-century charm offset by the thrusting bulk of a modern building in Long Street.

The narrow streets of the Bo-Kaap are lined with charming houses built, during the 18th century, for Cape Town's artisans. Emancipated slaves moved into the area in the 1830s, creating a Muslim enclave. *Above*: Pastel-coloured, flat-roofed dwellings are among the more striking of the district's diversity of architectural styles. *Right*: Vines and trailing plants embower one of the Bo-Kaap's Victorian houses.

Above: The view over the rooftops of the Bo-Kaap takes in Table Mountain and much of the City Bowl. The building with the wavy roof line at the far left is a national monument, and houses the Bo-Kaap Museum, a unique look into the heritage and way of life of the Muslim community. *Left*: Many of the Bo-Kaap's houses have been lovingly restored and display fine architectural detailing.

55

Aspects of the Bo-Kaap. *Left and below*: Among special days observed by the community is Rampisny, the birth of the Prophet Mohammed, when the women of the house fashion scented sachets from orange leaves. Celebrations begin when the men return from the mosque. *Right*: Music generally, and folk-songs in particular (traditional melodies with Afrikaans lyrics), is an integral part of social life. The residents of the Bo-Kaap form a close-knit community, bound together by their faith, and by traditions that go back to their Indonesian origins.

Infamous Island
& Portside Pastimes

Harbour construction in the early decades of the 20th century cut Capetonians off from their beloved seaside: gone were the pleasant, palm-fringed beachfront and much else, to be replaced by a concrete wilderness of functional buildings, grimy quaysides, barriers and tank farms. But much of the colour and vibrancy of the old days have returned; sea and city are united once again by the ambitious and highly successful Victoria & Alfred (V&A) Waterfront redevelopment scheme. Drawing its inspiration from harbour conversion projects in San Francisco, Sydney and elsewhere (but retaining a character, a certain stylishness very much its own), this imaginative enterprise has transformed the most venerable

portion of the harbour into an exuberant, appealing extravaganza of shopping malls, marinas and museums, restaurants and bistros, pubs, cinemas, nightclubs, cosy boutiques, speciality shops and craft emporia – a place of light, movement and music.

From the Waterfront, one can embark on a boat trip to Robben Island, which lies some 10 kilometres (6 miles) offshore in Table Bay. The low, oval-shaped island, just 574 hectares (1,418 acres) in extent, has a long history: early European navigators and the first white settlers hunted its penguins and seals (Robben means 'seals' in Dutch), collected the eggs of its seabirds and quarried its fine slate for their buildings. Over the years the island has functioned variously as a vast livestock pen, lunatic asylum, leper colony, military fortress and penal colony. Under the apartheid regime, Robben Island became a maximum security prison notorious for its harshness, its most illustrious resident Nelson Mandela. The island is now a nature reserve and museum, a poignant memorial to those who fought for, and eventually gained, a free country, and its fascinating history draws growing numbers of visitors each year.

Above: The Planet Hollywood theme restaurant brings a touch of Tinseltown to Africa's southern tip. ***Right***: The Waterfront in one of its more restful moods, showing some of the old dockyard buildings now converted to new purposes. Table Mountain provides a superlative backdrop.

Above: The stylish Table Bay Hotel is one of the finest additions to the V&A Waterfront's stable of world-class hotels. The Table Bay's logo (*right*) features a pair of Cape fur seals, often to be seen cavorting in the waters of the harbour. *Opposite*: The BMW Pavilion houses Africa's only IMAX cinema. *Overleaf*: Just metres from the Victoria Wharf shopping complex, the restless Atlantic hurls itself at the harbour defences.

Right: The silent magic of mime delights passers-by at the Waterfront. ***Below and opposite***: The New Year 'Coon Carnival' spills over into the Waterfront from its main venue in Green Point Stadium. The Cape 'coloured' community has a lively musical tradition: its songs, known as *gommaliedjies*, are drawn from a rich and eventful heritage. The cheerful, often racy numbers are performed at such gatherings as the 'Coon Carnival', in which scores of colourfully dressed minstrel troupes parade the city streets. The style and form owe something to old-time American minstrel shows, but the flavour is entirely Cape.

Top: By day, the Waterfront presents a panorama of activity; busy tugs and trawlers mingle with cruise and tour craft. *Above*: The Penny Ferry makes its four-minute trip between the Pierhead and South Quay. *Right*: The figurehead of the *Victoria*, a replica sailing vessel. *Far right*: In 1995, the Royal Yacht *Britannia* berthed at the Waterfront during Queen Elizabeth II's visit to South Africa.

Left: Chinese dragon-boat races have become a popular annual event at the Waterfront. Like the many ethnic and national holidays celebrated here, such events underline Cape Town's increasing status as one of the world's most cosmopolitan meeting places. *Overleaf*: The chilly waters of Table Bay are often the setting for exciting yacht and small-craft races. Highlights of the yachting scene are the annual Rothmans Week in Table Bay and the bi-annual Cape-to-Rio contest. Cape Town is also a stop on the gruelling Whitbread and BOC round-the-world races.

Previous pages: Robben Island, with Cape Town in the distance. On the left, the breakwaters of Murray's Harbour extend into Table Bay. Immediately to the right of the harbour lies the former political prison. Long a forbidden area to visitors, Robben Island now serves as both nature reserve and museum. *Opposite*: The lighthouse was built on Minto Hill in 1864. *Above*: The wreck of a Taiwanese fishing trawler, one of the numerous ships claimed by the island's jagged reefs. *Left*: A colony of jackass penguins is protected on the island.

Opposite, top: Of interest in Robben Island's tiny village is The Residency, once home to the island's commissioners and now a guest lodge. *Opposite, bottom*: The former Anglican church is now a multi-denominational house of worship. *Above*: Political prisoners performed hard labour in the island's lime quarry. The small cave visible in the quarry face provided both shelter and ablution facilities. In the foreground lies the symbolic pile of stones left behind by ex-prisoners when they revisited Robben Island in 1995. *Left*: Nelson Mandela re-creates, for reporters, the tedious work of stone-breaking.

Peninsular Perspectives

Beaches and blue sea feature prominently among the Cape Peninsula's attractions. The shoreline is scenically striking, graced by charming bays, high cliffs, hidden coves, lovely expanses of sand and by handsome little (some not so little) residential, fishing and resort centres that, in the warm summer months, entice holidaymakers, boating enthusiasts, scuba divers, swimmers, surfers and sunworshippers. There is surprising variety – in terms of both climate and terrain – along the 150-kilometre (94 miles) coast; ocean currents and the lie of the land combine to endow the two seaboards with entirely different characters.

The eastern or 'False Bay' side of the Peninsula, for instance, suffers the full force of the prevailing summer south-easter while the western, or Atlantic, strip remains, for the most part, pleasantly sheltered by mountains; the western waters are much colder than those of False Bay. The landscapes are at their most dramatic along the coastal road that leads southwards from the city suburbs of Sea Point, Clifton and Camps Bay to the seaside village of Llandudno. To travel along this route, at any time of the day but especially at the magical sunset hour, is delight indeed: on your left are the towering heights of the Twelve Apostles, on your right cliffs that tumble down to the rocks and pounding waves. Farther on, the road rises, cutting its way through Chapman's Peak in one of the country's most splendid scenic drives. The eastern coastal belt consists of a broad, sandy plain that meets the sea, without drama, in a great, curved band of golden beach that runs from Muizenberg to distant Gordon's Bay.

Above: Mouille Point's lighthouse, which dates from 1824, is the country's oldest coastal beacon.

Right: The rocky shores of Sea Point, one of the city's more densely populated and lively seaside suburbs. Its sociable promenade is much favoured by evening strollers.

Left: Although the appearance of the 'tablecloth' over Table Mountain and the Twelve Apostles signals that the south-easter is blowing, Clifton's sheltered beaches remain wind-free. These four secluded crescents of sand, girded by boulders, attract a fashionable crowd. The slopes above the shore are clustered with luxurious apartment blocks and villas. *Overleaf*: Clifton may be popular, but there is always room to be alone. The water here is usually clear, intensely blue, and very cold.

Right: Camps Bay, just along the coast from Clifton, is fringed by one of the Peninsula's most favoured beaches, a broad white expanse popular for family outings. Its palm-lined promenade and magnificent mountain backdrop add much to the ambience. *Below*: Beach activities range from this youngster's beach bats to high-profile international volleyball tournaments. *Bottom*: The Bay Hotel takes pride of place along Camps Bay's stylish seafront.

Roughly 10 kilometres (6 miles) along the rugged western coast from Camps Bay, and nestled in a wide valley, lies the town of Hout Bay. Because of its relative isolation from Cape Town, independent-minded locals refer jokingly to the town and its surrounds as the Republic of Hout Bay. *Previous pages*: Hout Bay's harbour, girded by mountains and filled with fishing boats. *Opposite, left and above:* The fishing community of Hout Bay is the hub of the Peninsula's cray-fishing industry. During June and July great numbers of snoek, a firm-fleshed and rather bony fish, are also caught off-shore and sold on the quayside.

The spacious aviaries at Hout Bay's World of Birds shelter more than 3 000

birds, from 450 or so different species. *Opposite*: A pair of crowned cranes.

Above: Greater flamingos.

A launch takes visitors on the short voyage from Hout Bay to Duiker Island, home to a large and lively colony of Cape fur seals. Several thousand of these frolicsome marine mammals, together with large numbers of cormorants, gather on the rocky little outcrop in the summer months.

The road south from Hout Bay leads along the flanks of Chapman's Peak, from which superlative vistas unfold – of the waters of the bay below, and of harbour, town and mountain in the distance. Chapman was an English mariner who landed, in 1607, to 'see whether it weare a harboure or not'.

The marine drive descends from Chapman's Peak to the marshy plain of Noordhoek and its 8-kilometre-long (5 miles) beach. *Left*: The sands, blown by a blustery wind, are often deserted and there are no seaside amenities, but it is a fine place for surfing, walking and for horseback riding (**below**). *Overleaf*: Further south from Noordhoek lies the village of Scarborough, which boasts another stretch of sandy beach much favoured by nature-lovers.

Images of Cape Point. *Above*: A stone cross honours the Portuguese navigator Bartholomeu Dias, first European to round the Cape of Good Hope, in 1487. *Below*: A rocky beach at the Cape of Good Hope. *Right*: The sensitively designed restaurant at Cape Point. *Opposite*: The old lighthouse at Cape Point is a superb lookout. *Overleaf*: The Peninsula is brought to an abrupt and dramatic end by the massive headland of Cape Point.

Cape Point lies within the 7,750-hectare (19,135 acres) Cape of Good Hope Nature Reserve, an expanse of heath-like fynbos vegetation renowned for its floral wealth: around 1,080 different species have been identified on the ridge of hills that runs down the False Bay side and on the undulating plain to the west. The rather bleak, treeless countryside is transformed when the wild flowers bloom, briefly, in late winter and spring.

The dead hulk of the Liberty ship *Thomas T Tucker*, wrecked in 1942 while carrying tanks and other war material to the Middle East, lies crumbling on the rocks near Olifantsbospunt, on the western shore of the Cape of Good Hope Nature Reserve. Cape Point's deadly combination of treacherous weather conditions, turbulent currents and jagged offshore reefs have claimed many vessels over the centuries.

Above and right: One of only two shore colonies of jackass penguins – a threatened species, named for its harsh, donkey-like call – can be seen and enjoyed at Boulders and nearby Foxy beaches near Simon's Town. *Top*: A mother keeps a watchful eye on her chick. The birds have quite happily adapted to their semi-urban habitat.

Behind Boulders Beach, shown in the foreground, are the outskirts of Simon's Town. This maritime centre was founded as an anchorage by, and named after, the able Cape colonial governor Simon van der Stel in 1687. For 150 years its dockyards served as the Royal Navy's principal South Atlantic base before reverting, in the 1950s, to South African control. Not surprisingly, the place is steeped in naval history.

Not too far down the coast from Simon's Town is the residential and resort village of St James, famed for the brightly painted bathing huts on its beachfront. Neighbouring Kalk Bay has a pretty little fishing harbour that is much visited by holidaymakers, especially during the winter months when the snoek are running. The catches are auctioned off, noisily and cheerfully, as soon as they are landed.

Left: Catamarans at rest on Fish Hoek beach. In summer, the ocean here is bright with the sails of leisure craft. Inland, in the valley that bisects the Peninsula, is the celebrated Peer's Cave, an important archaeological site that was home to 15 000-year old Fish Hoek Man. *Above*: Fishermen ready their craft for sea. *Overleaf*: Old-fashioned bathing huts lend a splash of colour to Muizenberg Beach.

As daylight fades over Table Bay, windsurfers ride the waves off Bl+oubergstrand, to the north of Cape Town. In the background, the famous 'tablecloth' tumbles off the summit of Table Mountain behind Lion's Head.

Above: Kiting enthusiasts go through their paces on the sands of Melkbosstrand ('milkwood beach'), on the coast some distance north of Cape Town. *Overleaf*: With the great pedestal of Table Mountain in the far distance, the dying embers of the day suffuse a dappled sky and the dunes of Bloubergstrand with a soft light.

A Foray
Southward

To the north and east of central Cape Town are the Cape Flats, a region that once lay under the ocean, separating what is now the Peninsula from the mainland. Today the sandy, windswept Flats support dense swathes of residential and industrial development and most of the region's informal settlements. Quite different in character are the longer established, leafy and affluent 'southern suburbs', a chain of one-time villages that hugs the lower slopes of the Table Mountain range and extends southwards along the rail line running from central Cape Town to Simon's Town. These are the oldest urban areas outside the city proper, originally founded as farms by the first 'free burghers' – men who left their jobs with the Dutch East India Company to strike out on their own in the mid-17th

century. The oldest of these suburbs is Rondebosch, where, in 1656, Dutch colonists first planted wheat. Among the grandest of the area's early buildings was Groote Schuur, or Great Barn, a large granary that was later extensively remodelled to become the official residence of South Africa's president and renamed Genadendal.

Of considerably more recent vintage are the suburb's two most striking features – the handsome University of Cape Town (UCT) and Rhodes Memorial. The medical faculty of UCT is internationally respected; its teaching arm, the huge Groote Schuur Hospital, was the venue for the first human heart transplant operation. Next-door Newlands is noted for its cricket and rugby grounds and for the exquisite gardens of Kirstenbosch, perhaps the loveliest corner of an area that has more than its share of beauty.

Above: The equestrian statue of 'Physical Energy' commands the view from Rhodes Memorial, on the lower slopes of Devil's Peak. *Right*: Rhodes Memorial commemorates Cecil John Rhodes, the 19th-century Cape premier, financial tycoon and eccentric visionary whose 'immense and brooding spirit' lay over so much of colonial Africa. The Grecian-type 'temple' is the work of his friend and personal architect, Herbert Baker.

116

Above: The University of Cape Town's upper campus, set on the eastern slopes of Table Mountain, on land bequeathed to the nation by Cecil Rhodes, provides fine views of the surrounding suburbs and mountains. *Right*: A puffing gargoyle stares out from a campus wall. *Opposite, bottom left*: Ivy-clad Fuller Hall, one of UCT's student residences. *Opposite, bottom right*: The university's Jameson Hall stands at the top of Jameson Steps.

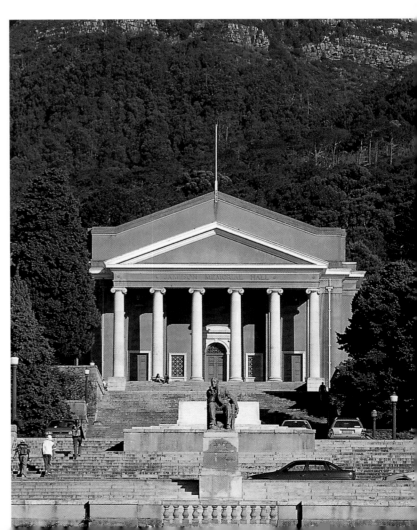

On the eastern slopes of Table Mountain lies Kirstenbosch National Botanical Garden, a broad expanse of well-watered land that sustains a profusion of indigenous plants. Among them are proteas and ericas, pelargoniums, succulents, ferns and cycads. A new conservatory, opened in 1998, displays desert and other species requiring specific climate conditions. *Opposite:* Spectacular displays of wild flowers herald the arrival of spring. *Above:* The Protea Garden is justly celebrated for its many varieties of protea. *Left:* The shaded restaurant area is a favourite lunch venue.

A trio of Kirstenbosch's exquisite flowering plants. *Right*: The red disa, *Disa uniflora*, is also known as the Pride of Table Mountain. This orchid blooms during the three months after Christmas. *Below*: *Mimetes fimbrifolius*, a variety of protea that is found only within the Cape Peninsula. *Opposite*: *Erica discolor*, one of South Africa's 612 species of erica, many of which have clusters of bell-like pendant flowers.

The grounds of Kirstenbosch are graced by an enchanting array of proteas, a family and genus of flowering plant named after Proteus, the mythological Greek god who could change his shape at will (the plants are enormously varied in form, size and habit). South Africa is home to 69 species of this intriguing family. *Right*: The king protea, the country's national flower, has the largest flowerhead of all. This floral wealth is a magnet for the nectar-eating Cape sugarbird (*above*), the scarlet-breasted sunbird (*left*) and many others.

The floral displays at Kirstenbosch are concentrated within 40 hectares (16 acres) of cultivated ground in a series of gardens graced by natural features, rockeries, terraces and broad walkways, like the one shown above. The sections are arranged in specialized spreads that include, among others, the protea gardens and a rock garden; a 'Braille walk' and perfume garden have been created for the visually challenged.

Tree ferns shade Kirstenbosch's enchanting Dell, site of the bird-shaped stone pool built by Colonel Bird, original owner of the land on which the gardens were laid out in 1913. The surrounding Cycad Amphitheatre is haven to a splendid collection of cycads, species that trace their ancestry to ancient seed-bearing flora that flourished between 60 and 50 million years ago – that is, before the appearance of flowering plants.

A waterfall in the Newlands Forest typifies the sylvan beauty of this corner of the southern suburbs. The forests that girdle the lower slopes of the Table Mountain range are much favoured by hikers, strollers and nature-lovers.

Of Vines & Gables

Towards the south the woodland slopes of the Table Mountain range descend to a beautiful valley, a broad swathe of fertile land granted to the Cape colonial governor Simon van der Stel in 1685 and later divided up into six farms. Here Van der Stel built his country retreat, a simple homestead which he named Groot Constantia and which, over the succeeding generations, changed and grew to become one of the stateliest of the Western Cape's historic mansions. Later, Hendrik Cloete enlarged the house, widened its facade, added gables and built a splendid wine cellar. Cloete also pioneered the Constantia valley's vineyards to produce wines of legendary quality that were much in demand in Europe. Sadly, the Cloete wine-making secrets have been lost, but the valley's wine estates still produce excellent vintages. Groot Constantia was virtually destroyed by fire in 1925, but the building has been beautifully restored to its former grandeur. An elegant, single-storey, U-shaped homestead, it is an example of Cape Dutch architecture at its classic best.

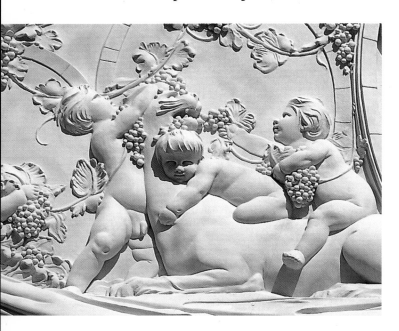

Several other Constantia valley farmsteads have also survived the centuries with honour. Alphen, for instance, is an exclusive country hotel. Groot Constantia is perhaps the most famous portion of a wine route – the only one in the Peninsula – rounded out by Buitenverwachting and Klein Constantia, and by the Steenberg estate, one of the valley's earliest farms.

Constantia is also known as one of the country's most exclusive addresses, with many of its lavish homes changing hands for millions. Entrancing tracts of forest grace the upper slopes of the valley, with the Cecilia Forest arguably the loveliest. The nearby Constantia Nek restaurant is a much-loved local institution, and occupies the saddle that divides the Constantia valley from neighbouring Hout Bay valley.

Above: A detail from the carved pediment of Groot Constantia's wine cellar. *Right*: The facade of Groot Constantia, one of the earliest and grandest of the country's Cape Dutch homesteads.

Right: The striking pediment of Groot Constantia's double-storey wine cellar, an elaborate stucco relief carved by the French-born sculptor Anton Anreith, shows Ganymede, cup-bearer to the gods, surrounded by exuberant cherubs. *Below*: Buitenverwachting's green and pleasant grounds. ***Opposite, top***: The historic Alphen homestead is now a sophisticated hotel.

Serried ranks of vines mantle the slopes of the Constantia valley, their bounty yielding superb wines. *Opposite*: Buitenverwachting and some of its vineyards. The estate is known for its excellent restaurant. *Above*: Klein Constantia, an old homestead rescued from decay through the efforts of a local businessman. *Overleaf*: With its vineyards, forest plantations and expansive villas, the Constantia valley is decidedly rural in appearance.

Wine, Whales & Wild Flowers

Beyond the Cape Flats, to the north and east, lie the grand mountain ranges and fertile valleys of the Cape winelands, a region blessed with both abundance and great beauty. The winelands were the first of the rural areas to be occupied by the early European settlers: they began moving away from Cape Town and into the traditional grazing lands of the indigenous Khoikhoi people in the 1660s, marking out their farms, planting first wheat and then grapevines, building homesteads, and establishing small settlements – Stellenbosch and Franschhoek, Paarl, Tulbagh, Wellington and others – that have grown gracefully over the centuries. The legacy seduces the senses: the immediate hinterland and, farther out, the luxuriant valleys of the Breede and Berg rivers, are infinite in their scenic variety, enchanting in all their seasons. Springtime

decorates the hedgerows, the fields and hillsides with wild flowers; in summer the vineyards and orchards are heavy with fruit, the air filled with the scents of the harvests; autumn clothes the landscapes in warm russets and golds; snow covers the high peaks in winter.

No less attractive in its own way is the countryside to the east, across the Hottentots-Holland Mountains. The region, known as the Overberg, is noted for the rugged cliffs, the beaches, coves and bays of its shoreline, and for the rich wheat and barley fields, green pastures, forest plantations and gentle charm of the inland areas. Biggest of its coastal centres is Hermanus, famed for the great southern right whales that come into its bay to mate and to calve.

Very different is the western coastal belt, whose waters sustain a major part of the country's fishing industry. Here the soils become poorer the farther north one travels, the shoreline bleaker, the land drier. But the region has its appeal – most notably after the winter rains, when the sandveld ephemerals cloak the landscapes in glorious carpets of colour.

Above: Massive oak vats line the cellars of Nederburg, venue of the country's premier wine auction.
Right: Autumn colours mantle maturing vines in the valley beneath the Klein Drakenstein range.

Filigreed wrought ironwork decorates the facade of the venerable Oom Samie se Winkel. Dating back to 1904, this general dealer is a longstanding fixture of picturesque Dorp Street in Stellenbosch.

The interior of Oom Samie se Winkel is a veritable Aladdin's cave of delights, ranging from tools and hardware to apparel, spices and fine wines. A leafy courtyard behind the shop boasts a pleasant tea garden.

A favourite lunch venue for Capetonians
and visitors alike is Boschendal, a Cape
Flemish-style homestead located near
Stellenbosch. *Above*: Boschendal's shady
grounds are perfect for picnicking.
Right: The estate's elegant gazebo.
Opposite: The manor house, built in
1812, deteriorated in the later 1800s but
was rescued and restored to serve as a
museum, restaurant and centrepiece of a
splendid wine farm. *Overleaf*: The flour-
ishing vineyards of the Franschhoek
Valley are the legacy of the Huguenot
(French Protestant) families who settled
this mountain-girt valley towards the
end of the 17th century.

142

Strawberries are grown, picked and sold from farm stalls along the roads around Stellenbosch. *Above*: The imaginatively contrived scarecrows who mutely watch over the strawberry fields have become landmarks around Stellenbosch. *Opposite, bottom*: A mother and her son pick strawberries at the Polkadraai farmstall. *Overleaf*: Afternoon sunshine bathes a winelands farmstead in soft light.

Hermanus, roughly two hours' drive east of Cape Town, is among the southern hemisphere's premier whale-watching areas, renowned for the southern rights that mate and calve in the waters of Walker Bay from June through to November. *Previous pages*: The rocks that fringe Walker Bay at Hermanus offer superb vantage points for whale-watching. *Opposite*: Craft markets are a feature of the annual Hermanus whale festival held in September. *Above*: The town's professional whale crier, Pieter Claasen, heralds the arrival of the great marine mammals.

Club Mykonos, a time-share and holiday complex inspired by the Greek Isles, lies just outside Langebaan on the West Coast. *Above*: A donkey and his master evoke visions of the Mediterranean. *Right*: Guests stay in white-washed colourfully trimmed apartments known as *kalifas*; streets are cobbled.

SAS SALDANHA
NATURE TRAILS
                    14.5 KM
RED   11 KM
YELLOW   9.5 KM
GREEN   4 KM

Left: A myriad springtime flowers bring brief colour to the sandveld terrain near Saldanha Bay. The region north of the Olifants River, known as Namaqualand, is home to more than 4 000 floral species, most belonging to the daisy and mesembryanthemum groups although others – succulents, aloes, lilies and perennial herbs – are well represented. *Overleaf*: A seaside chapel in the fishing village of Paternoster.